For Maria Furriols, a great mountain lover.
MIA

This book was finished during the 2020 lockdown.
It's my humble tribute to the incredible places just waiting for us.
For Maddi and Adur, who will soon be able to travel through color.
MARCOS

Published in 2022 by Orange Mosquito
An Imprint of Welbeck Children's Limited
part of Welbeck Publishing Group.
Based in London and Sydney.
www.welbeckpublishing.com

In collaboration with Mosquito Books Barcelona S.L.

© Mosquito Books Barcelona, SL 2022
Text © Mia Cassany 2022
Illustration © Marcos Navarro 2022
Translation: Clare Gaunt
Publisher: Margaux Durigon
Production: Jess Brisley

ISBN: 9781914519307
eISBN: 9781914519314

Printed in India
10 9 8 7 6 5 4 3 2 1

FSC
MIX
Paper
FSC® C020056

MAJESTIC MOUNTAINS

Discover Earth's Mighty Peaks

ORANGE
M·O·S·Q·U·I·T·O

MIA CASSANY · MARCOS NAVARRO

CRATER LAKE

NORTH AMERICA

YOSEMITE

WHITE SANDS NATIONAL PARK

ARENAL VOLCANO

MOUNT RORAIMA

MACHU PICCHU

SOUTH AMERICA

ANTARCTICA

Mountain ecosystems are found all over the earth, from Ecuador to the North and South Poles. They cover approximately one-fifth of the land on our planet. As well as being breathtakingly beautiful, these magnificent places are vital for a balanced world. Their fauna and flora are fundamental to the harmony of

WORLD'S MOUNTAINS

ARCTIC

LANDMANNALAUGAR

ASIA

EUROPE

ALTAI MOUNTAINS

MONTE PERDIDO

MONT BLANC

MOUNT FUJI

ZHANGJIAJIE

MOUNT EVEREST

CHOCOLATE HILLS

AFRICA

MOUNT KILIMANJARO

BUNGLE BUNGLE RANGE

ANTARCTICA

the entire planet. Mountains are a great source of drinking water. And their plants produce lots of the oxygen we need to breathe. And did you know mountains can move? Every year, tectonic plate movements inch our mountains forward (and sometimes upward!) by just a few inches.

MACHU PICCHU, PERU

Peru is home to one of the world's most famous mountains: Machu Picchu. Locals have spoken the language, Quechua, for over a thousand years in this spectacular part of South America. And in Quechua, Machu Picchu means Old Mountain. In 2000, it was named one of the New Seven Wonders of the World.

Machu Picchu is a sacred place. Incredibly, its citadel was built on a crest of the mountain. This archaeological site is incredibly important to our understanding of the Incas, a hugely successful pre-Colombian empire.

To reach the summit, you have to climb the Inca Trail. It is full of steep paths and tricky climbs. Unless you are a llama, alpaca, or guanaco, getting up this mountain is no easy feat!

MOUNT EVEREST, THE HIMALAYA MOUNTAIN RANGE

The awe-inspiring Himalayas lie along the border between China and Nepal. This iconic range is home to the world's tallest mountain—and also the world's most famous peak.

Standing at no less than 29,029 feet above sea level, this magnificent mountain has an extreme climate. Temperatures generally measure around -22º Fahrenheit in winter, and can go as low as -94º Fahrenheit! Couple that with very strong winds, and only a few plants and animals can survive here.

Yaks however are well-adapted to these steep slopes. They live off a kind of lichen—one of the few plants that can survive this far up.

MOUNT FUJI, JAPAN

The ultra-famous and sensationally beautiful volcano, Mount Fuji, towers over central Japan from its position on the main island of Honshu. It is venerated as one of the country's national icons.

Although scientists think it is still active, the risk of this volcano erupting is actually very low. The mountain's full name is Fu-Ji-San, which means wealth, samurai, and mountain in Japanese. Locals refer to it as Mihanaro which stands for 3,776, its total height in meters (the equivalent of ~2,388 feet). Making it Japan's highest summit!

Because of this high altitude, the peak is very cold; making it hard for vegetation to recover and grow between freezes. But the skirts (bottom) of Mount Fuji are home to lush forests.

There is no doubt it is one of the most recognizable mountains in the world.

SEARCH & FIND
24
ANIMALS!

YOSEMITE, USA

California's Sierra Nevada is home to one of the United States' most gorgeous locations: Yosemite National Park.

Huge numbers of visitors come here every year. They tend to stay in the vast valley, but the park has so much more to explore! It is full of awe-inspiring cliffs, stunning waterfalls, tall forests, and lakes with crystal-clear water. And that's before mentioning some of the magnificent mountains that can be found here: El Capitán is the most famous peak in the park. It measures 2,986 feet high and its spectacular rock faces are formed out of granite.

The American black bear is one of the park's lucky residents. Although these large animals seem hefty and ungainly, they're actually very agile hunters. They can tunnel into the soil and even climb trees.

SEARCH & FIND
20
ANIMALS!

MOUNT MAZAMA, CRATER LAKE, USA

Mount Mazama forms part of the Cascade Range, a collection of mountains found in the Crater Lake National Park, in the state of Oregon, USA.

Over 7,000 years ago, an extremely violent eruption triggered the collapse of the entire mountain. The crater it left in the surface (known as a caldera) gradually cooled down and filled with rain. This long process created a fabulously intense blue pool of clear water, which we call Crater Lake.

The area is home to an incredible variety of birds. It really would be amazing to be able to soar like a bird over this natural wonder and observe it from the air.

CHOCOLATE HILLS, PHILIPPINES

To truly appreciate this unique mountain landscape, you need to visit Bohol Island. Over 1,000 conical hills are packed into around 19.3 square miles of land. Their striking similarity looks almost manmade.

Usually, the hills are green with thick vegetation. But during the dry season, from December to May, there is very little rain and all the plants dry out. The landscape turns brown and the vista starts to resemble a giant bar of chocolate.

Experts believe this mountain formation started growing beneath the sea millions of years ago. Eventually, it pushed through the surface. After another few thousand years, the wind and weather had molded it into unusual mounds.

MONT BLANC, FRANCE – ITALY

The Alps are a chain of European mountains, spanning the borders between France, Italy, Switzerland, Austria, Germany, Liechtenstein, and Slovenia.

Mont Blanc is the highest peak in the range. Its imposing summit is surrounded by glaciers and reaches up to 15,780 feet. Such altitude means it is covered in snow all year round. Its name translates into White Mountain. Covered in delightful alpine vegetation, these slopes are also home to thousands of big and little beasts.

One of these, the male Alpine ibex, is a kind of wild goat with strong, oversized horns. During the mating season, the ibex perform gravity-defying leaps and rear up on their back legs to increase their push power, and to fight off their competition.
It is an incredible sight.

SEARCH & FIND
5
ANIMALS!

SEARCH & FIND
19
ANIMALS!

ZHANGJIAJIE, CHINA

The vast Zhangjiajie National Forest Park is in the north of Hunan province in China.
It is part of the Wulingyuan Scenic Area—a UNESCO World Heritage Site.
The first of China's national forest parks, it is protected for its
outstanding beauty—it is a uniquely special place.

Zhangjiajie's many mountains have an unusual shape; sheer rock columns that spike
the sky. Over 3,100 pillar formations are ensconced in rich vegetation. And some of
them reach over 3,300 feet high. A few of these incredible structures stand alone
in the middle of open space, creating a unique, spectacular landscape.

The surrounding jungle is home to fascinating fauna like the
pangolin, one of the most interesting animals on earth.

MOUNT RORAIMA, VENEZUELA-BRAZIL

Mount Roraima is the highest point of the Pacaraima Mountains in South America.

It is a table-top mountain or tepui, famous for its unique shape. Tepuis have a flat top, instead of the more usual pointy mountain peak with cone-shaped sides; and Roraima's cliff-faces drop straight down over some 1,300 feet on each side. Incredible!

Because this mountain has such a special shape, the animals and plants that live here are unique too. It is almost impossible to find them anywhere else. Roraima is home to spectacular carnivorous plants and the endemic (native to a specific area) frogs and butterflies brave enough to live among them.

SEARCH & FIND
49
ANIMALS!

SEARCH & FIND
14
ANIMALS!

MOUNT KILIMANJARO, TANZANIA

Africa's tallest mountain is Mount Kilimanjaro. It is located in northeast Tanzania, near the Kenyan border.

No other mountain in the world is like this one—it is a triple-peaked volcano! In other words, it was created by three eruptions. Shira, the oldest crater, is on the left, followed by Kibo in the middle and Mawenzi on the right. The volcano is now dormant.

One of Kilimanjaro's spectacular features are the ice fields around the summit. Sadly these are disappearing under the influence of global warming.

Mount Kilimanjaro has been protected for many years, partly to care for its magnificent animals. It is a forest reserve where hunting is banned. It is important to respect and conserve one of the most extraordinary places on the planet.

ARENAL VOLCANO, COSTA RICA

The little town of La Fortuna is the gateway to the enormous Arenal Volcano.
In 1968, this volcano decided to surprise the world with a colossal eruption.

It continued spitting out tons of lava until 2010, sending rocks and stones flying at speeds of over 75 miles per hour.

Although Arenal is now in a resting phase, you can still spot plenty of signs of volcanic activity: ash columns, loud underground noises, tiny flows of hot orange lava that still haven't cooled, a few explosions, unusual heat...it really is a powerful mountain!

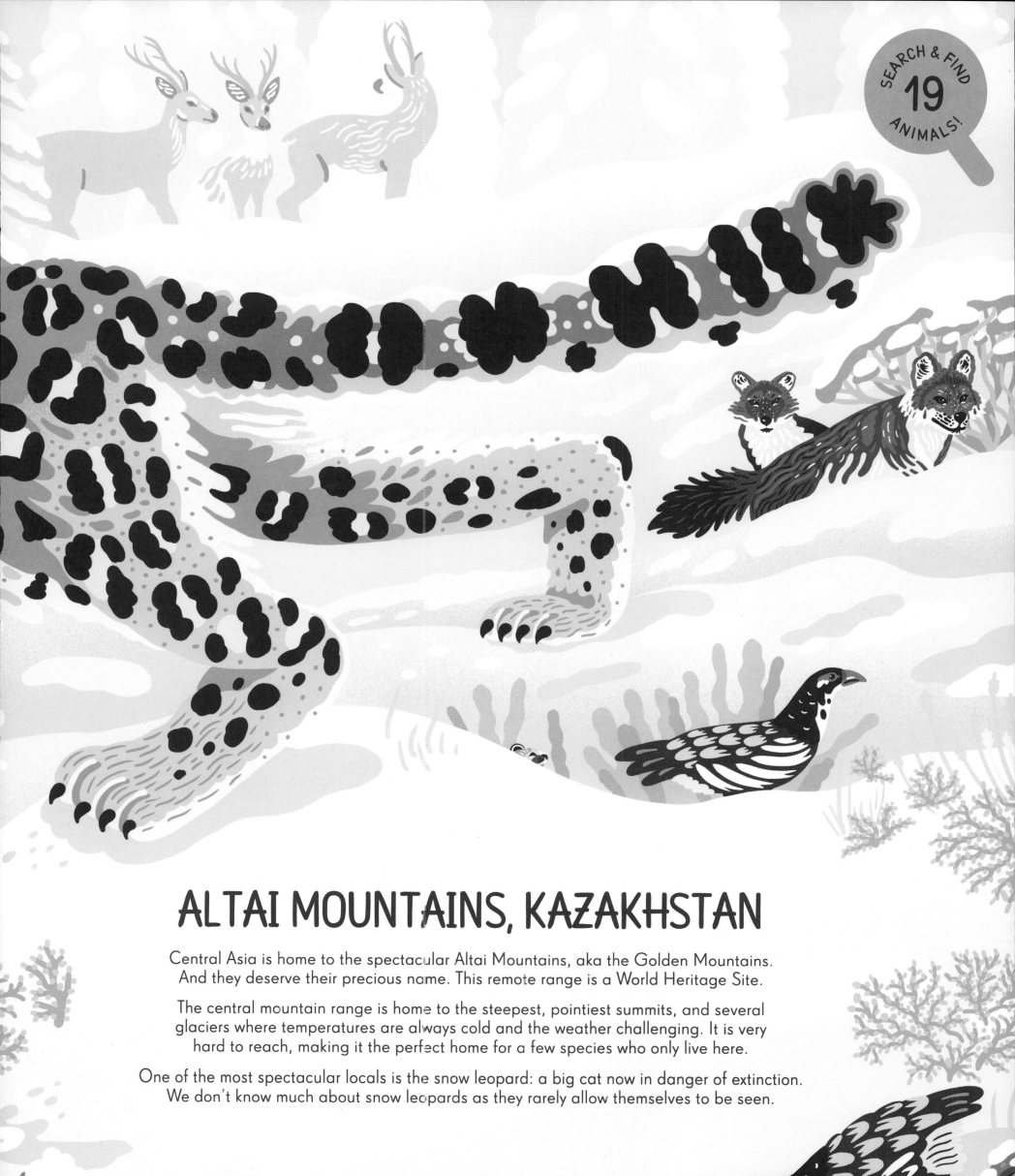

ALTAI MOUNTAINS, KAZAKHSTAN

Central Asia is home to the spectacular Altai Mountains, aka the Golden Mountains. And they deserve their precious name. This remote range is a World Heritage Site.

The central mountain range is home to the steepest, pointiest summits, and several glaciers where temperatures are always cold and the weather challenging. It is very hard to reach, making it the perfect home for a few species who only live here.

One of the most spectacular locals is the snow leopard: a big cat now in danger of extinction. We don't know much about snow leopards as they rarely allow themselves to be seen.

WHITE SANDS NATIONAL PARK, USA

There's an area of Southern New Mexico filled with little white sand dunes. It is a stunning landscape.

White dazzles your eyes, because the land is made up of gypsum crystals. This glistening mineral is commonly found in several types of rocks. The wind helps erode the rock, turning it into tiny grains of white sand, and then blows them into little mounds.

Experts have found fossilized human footprints and animal prints dating all the way back to the Ice Age!

BUNGLE BUNGLE RANGE, AUSTRALIA

The mountains in this striking range are found in the Purnululu National Park. The rounded cones resemble beehive-shaped towers with their bands "printed" in a gorgeous range of oranges and reds.

These beautiful formations are actually made up of several layers of different stone, all piled up on top of each other. The layers containing the highest levels of humidity look darker, while the more mineral-rich rocks look brighter.

SEARCH & FIND 10 ANIMALS!

SEARCH & FIND
24
ANIMALS!

MONTE PERDIDO, SPAIN

Spain's highest limestone massif lurks in the Central Pyrenees, in the province of Huesca.

The seasons can be extreme, with periods of dry cold weather giving way
to warmer, more welcoming temperatures in the summer.

This mountain is an important home for lots of birds, including a range of spectacular owl species. These nocturnal birds are a good example of how life changes in the mountains. During the day, the place feels practically uninhabited and there are few animals to be seen. But when it gets dark, you start to hear little noises, glimpse the sparkling reflection of a pair of eyes, hear twigs crackling underfoot, along with the odd hoot...it is nighttime!

LANDMANNALAUGAR, ICELAND

The Highlands of Iceland are home to a hidden paradise. The landscape is practically untouched, and scattered with incredibly beautiful, brightly colored mountains. It is a dreamy—and steamy—place; as geothermal hot springs are formed by water coming up to the surface from deep underground.

Filled with glaciers, the odd volcano, snow, frozen rivers...and lava fields, this magnificent location is home to mountains in all kinds of colors. Fluorescent green moss makes everything look surprisingly unnatural.

WANT TO LEARN MORE?

 The number of times this creature appears on the page.

Discover more about some of these wonderful creatures.

MACHU PICCHU, PERU

- 2 Guanacos *(Lama guanicoe)*
- 1 Vicuña *(Vicugna vicugna)*
- 4 Alpacas *(Vicugna pacos)*
- 9 Llamas *(Lama glama)*
- 2 Andean condors *(Vultur gryphus)*

Guanaco, vicuña, alpaca, and llama are all types of South American camelid, which makes them part of the camel and dromedary family. All of the members of the same herd poop in the same place. They decide on a particular spot and make it their bathroom!

MOUNT EVEREST, THE HIMALAYA MOUNTAIN RANGE

- 3 Himalayan jumping spiders *(Euophrys omnisuperstes)*
- 2 Wild yaks *(Bos mutus)*
- 1 Himalayan pika *(Ochotona himalayana)*
- 4 Red pandas *(Ailurus fulgens)*
- 5 Himalayan tahrs *(Hemitragus jemlahicus)*
- 2 Alpine choughs *(Pyrrhocorax graculus)*

YAK
This huge animal has enormous lungs, allowing it to breathe easily at high altitudes. Yaks are also incredibly strong. They can carry up to 220 pounds without struggling, so Sherpas (skillful Himalayan mountain guides) use them to take climbing gear up the steep slopes.

RED PANDA
Red pandas are roughly the same size as a cat, look a bit like raccoons, and have an enormous tail. Shy and solitary, they generally only come down from the safety of the trees to find food.

HIMALAYAN JUMPING SPIDER
This tiny wee insect lives among the Himalayan rocks. It is the earth's highest permanent resident, surviving on tiny bits of vegetation and the few insects blown up the mountains by the wind.

MOUNT FUJI, AOKIGAHARA

- 3 Citrus long-horned beetles (*Anoplophora chinensis*)
- 1 Asian black bear (*Ursus thibetanus*)
- 2 Small Japanese moles (*Mogera imaizumii*)
- 3 Japanese squirrels (*Sciurus lis*)
- 3 Silver-washed fritillary butterflies (*Argynnis paphia*)
- 5 Holly blue butterflies (*Celastrina argiolus*)
- 3 Pallas' sailer butterflies (*Neptis sappho*)
- 1 Japanese serow (*Capricornis crispus*)
- 2 Japanese paradise flycatchers (*Terpsiphone atrocaudata*)
- 1 Grey wagtail (*Motacilla cinerea*)

JAPANESE SEROW

These very peaceful animals like to be by themselves. And although they may not look it, they're actually very agile and can climb, jump and scale terrifyingly high cliffs! The male serow performs a funny dance to attract a mate. They bash their front legs against their hind legs repeatedly!

MOLE
Contrary to common thought, these fascinating animals aren't blind! However, their tiny eyes don't allow them to see very much, so they use their incredibly sensitive sense of smell to guide them around and find tasty worms to eat.

ASIAN BLACK BEAR
The Asian Black Bear is the smallest member of the bear family. The white chevron on their chest and more orangey patches of fur make them easy to tell apart from their cousins. Powerful claws make them really great hunters.

YOSEMITE, USA

SIERRA NEVADA BIGHORN SHEEP
These animals look a lot like common goats... except for their spectacular horns. The males engage in annual epic battles to win themselves a mate.

- 2 California ground squirrels (*Otospermophilus beecheyi*)
- 3 Western gray squirrels (*Sciurus griseus*)
- 2 Douglas squirrels (*Tamiasciurus douglasii*)
- 3 American black bears (*Ursus americanus*)
- 1 Coyote (*Canis latrans*)
- 2 White-headed woodpeckers (*Leuconotopicus albolarvatus*)
- 2 Steller's jays (*Cyanocitta stelleri*)
- 3 Clark's nutcrackers (*Nucifraga columbiana*)
- 2 Sierra Nevada Bighorn Sheep
  (*Ovis canadensis sierrae*)

COYOTE
The color of a coyote's fur can vary greatly, from white to brown, depending on where it lives. Coyotes are expert, super-fast night hunters. They make a huge range of different sounds, from shrieks to growls via howls and even barking!

MOUNT MAZAMA, CRATER LAKE

- 3 Peregrine falcons (*Falco peregrinus*)
- 3 American dippers (*Cinclus mexicanus*)
- 3 Common ravens (*Corvus corax*)
- 3 Canada jays (*Perisoreus canadensis*)
- 5 Bald eagles (*Haliaeetus leucocephalus*)
- 7 Canada gees (*Branta canadensis*)

BALD EAGLE
Bald eagles are spectacular looking birds, and expert predators. Their outstanding vision and powerful claws make it easy for them to hunt. In spite of their name, they aren't actually bald. Instead, their heads are colored in lovely white feathers. Part of their mating ritual involves flying at each other at top speed, grabbing their partner by the claws, and plummeting several yards, while spinning around together in the sky. It is an unbelievable performance!

CHOCOLATE HILLS, PHILIPPINES

🔍

- ○ 3 Philippine tarsiers *(Carlito syrichta)*
- ● 4 Javanese grasshoppers *(Valanga nigricornis)*

PHILIPPINE TARSIER
These funny little animals are the smallest member of the primate family and can fit into the palm of your hand. They use ultrasound to communicate, so we can't hear them! Scientists used to believe they were one of the world's most silent creatures. But careful observation showed deliberate, conscious, forceful opening of their eyes and mouths, which suggests they spend the whole day shouting! Their pitch is simply too high for us to notice.

MONT BLANC, FRANCE-ITALY

🔍

- ● 1 Bearded vulture *(Gypaetus barbatus)*
- ● 2 Alpine ibex *(Capra ibex)*
- ○ 1 Northern goshawk *(Accipiter gentilis)*
- ○ 1 Golden eagle *(Aquila chrysaetos)*

ALPINE IBEX
Alpine ibex are fantastic climbers, capable of ascending the steepest mountains. They use even the tiniest bits of rock jutting out from the cliff face as footholds, which allows them to reach summits with ease.

STEJNEGER'S PIT VIPER
Unusually, these snakes come out at night in order to avoid the heat of the day. Their patience saves energy, as they wait quietly for their prey to get close enough to catch.

ZHANGJIAJIE, CHINA

🔍

- ● 3 Crested myna birds *(Acridotheres cristatellus)*
- ● 2 Chinese pangolin *(Manis pentadactyla)*
- ● 1 Stejneger's pit viper *(Trimeresurus stejnegeri)*
- ● 7 Spotted lanternfly *(Lycorma delicatula)*
- ○ 3 Butterflies
- ○ 3 Butterflies
- ○ COLONY OF ANTS

CHINESE PANGOLIN
Pangolins are truly unique animals. They are the only mammal covered in scales, and their tongue can be longer than their entire body! When they feel threatened, pangolins curl up into a ball and roll out of danger. This happens a lot. They don't like being held in captivity and are in a constant state of alert. They sometimes even die of stress!

MOUNT RORAIMA, VENEZUELA-BRAZIL

🔍

- ○ 7 Roraima black frogs (*Oreophrynella quelchii*)
- ● 8 Pebble toads (*Oreophrynella nigra*)
- ● 1 Tarantula
- ● 8 Mariposa negra (*Pedaliodes roraimae*)
- ● 7 Brown-breasted antpitta (*Myrmothera simplex*)
- ○ 5 Tepui goldenthroats (*Polytmus milleri*)
- ● 2 Greater flowerpiercers (*Digiossa major*)
- ● 6 Straight-billed hermits (*Phaethornis bourcieri*)
- ● 5 Beetles

TARANTULA
The world's largest spider spreads out its legs to make itself look even bigger when it feels threatened. It needs to shed its exoskeleton (a skeleton outside the body) as it grows. Its skin is so fragile that, without this protective outer layer, even a low fall could lead to instant death.

STRAIGHT-BILLED HERMIT
These birds only live in humid climates. Their favorite food is pollen from the plants and flowers that grow in their environment.

MOUNT KILIMANJARO, TANZANIA

🔍

- ● 3 African bush elephants (*Loxodonta africana*)
- ○ 2 Masai giraffes (*Giraffa camelopardalis tippelskirchii*)
- ● 3 White-browed robin-chats (*Cossypha heuglini*)
- ○ 6 Dimorphic egrets (*Egretta dimorpha*)

AFRICAN BUSH ELEPHANT
An African elephant's enormous ears help to keep it cool, and are also used for communication. The lines on its ears are a bit like fingerprints: no two patterns are identical! Their trunks are a great nose, and they're also useful for grabbing food, sucking up water, pushing things around, and even for having a good scratch!

GIRAFFE
It is hard to see when a giraffe is sleeping because they only snooze standing up, and from between ten minutes to two hours a day!

ARENAL VOLCANO, COSTA RICA

🔍

- ○ 4 Hoffmann's two-toed sloths (*Choloepus hoffmanni*)
- ● 1 Geoffroy's spider monkey (*Ateles geoffroyi*)
- ○ 1 Mantled howler (*Alouatta palliata*)
- ● 4 Panamanian white-faced (*Cebus imitator*)
- ○ 4 Yellow-throated toucans (*Ramphastos ambiguus*)

YELLOW-THROATED TOUCAN
These special, gorgeous birds have enormous beaks that they use to keep their bodies cool in warm climates. Baby toucans grow beaks before they are two months old!

SLOTH
Contrary to popular belief, sloths are not primates! These extremely slow animals spend all their energy digesting food, leaving only just enough to allow them to move. Their gigantic claws are great for hanging from the trees.

ALTAI MOUNTAINS, KAZAKHSTAN

🔍
- 1 Snow leopard (*Panthera uncia*)
- 2 Tian Shan dhole (*Cuon alpinus hesperius*)
- 3 Elks (*Alces alces*)
- 4 Alpine pikas (*Ochotona alpina*)
- 3 Altai snowcocks (*Tetraogallus altaicus*)
- 3 Siberian roe deer (*Capreolus altaicus*)
- 3 Black kites (*Milvus migrans*)

ALPINE PIKA
This adorable animal is a little herbivorous mammal. They're constantly on the move, never still, and always about to run away!

WHITE SANDS NATIONAL PARK, USA

🔍
- 2 Lesser earless lizards (*Holbrookia maculata*)
- 5 Plains pocket mice (*Perognathus flavescens*)
- 3 Kangaroo rats (*Dipodomys*)
- 1 Whites and sensis moth (*Protogygia whitesandsensis*)
- 1 North American porcupine (*Erethizon dorsatum*)
- 5 Bleached skimmers (*Libellula composita*)
- 3 Sand scorpion (*Paruroctonus utahensis*)
- 2 Stohecker's sand-treader crickets (*Daihiniodes larvale*)
- 14 Tegeticula elatella moths (*Tegeticula elatella*)
- 2 Beach wolf spiders (*Arctosa littoralis*)
- 2 Kit foxes (*Vulpes macrotis*)
- 2 Black-tailed jackrabbits (*Lepus californicus*)
- 1 *Chihuahuan raven* (*Corvus cryptoleucus*)
- 3 Greater roadrunners (*Geococcyx californianus*)
- 4 Darkling beetles (*Eleodes obscurus sulcipennis*)

PORCUPINE
Porcupines are born with spines. They come out soft, but take only a few hours to harden.

KIT FOX
The kit fox has to live in sandy places, because that's where it digs its dens. Several entrances to their deep labyrinths are built for safety.

GREATER ROADRUNNER
Unlike other birds, the roadrunner speeds along the ground. It is capable of flying and gliding, but it only travels short distances in the air—using its tail as a rudder.

BUNGLE BUNGLE RANGE, AUSTRALIA

🔍
- 4 Emus (*Dromaius novaehollandiae*)
- 2 White-quilled rock pigeons (*Petrophassa albipennis*)
- 2 Agile wallabies (*Macropus agilis*)
- 2 Brush-tailed rock wallabies (*Kangurus penicillatus*)

AGILE WALLABY
Wallabies aren't kangaroos—they're smaller. But like their cousins, they have very strong back legs, which are great for jumping around and defending themselves. Wallabies belong to the marsupial family, in which all females have a pouch to carry their babies.

ELK

Elk are solitary animals that like cold regions. You can't mistake their huge antlers, although the females have slightly smaller versions than the male. Both genders shed their antlers each year. And every pair of antlers is different, which makes individuals easy to identify.

SNOW LEOPARD

Although the snow leopard is a member of the big cat family, it can't roar.

MONTE PERDIDO, SPAIN

- 1 Beech marten *(Martes foina)*
- 1 Ferret *(Mustela putorius furo)*
- 2 Tawny owls *(Strix aluco)*
- 4 Boreal owls *(Aegolius funereus)*
- 2 Eurasian scops owl *(Otus scops)*
- 7 Giant peacock moths *(Saturnia pyri)*
- 7 Alpine long-eared bats *(Plecotus macrobullaris)*

Owls are incredible. They can turn their head through 270 degrees in both directions! And their powerful claws are great for hunting. Many owls have feathery tips on either side of their head which they use to show how they're feeling. People think these are ears, but they're wrong!

ALPINE LONG-EARED BAT

These bats have massive ears! Unusually, the females are bigger than the males. Bats are nocturnal animals and are practically blind. So they use extremely precise ultrasound to calculate their distance from the things around them.

LANDMANNALAUGAR, ICELAND

- 11 Icelandic horses *(Equus ferus caballus)*

ICELANDIC HORSE

Icelandic horses are the only animal originally from Iceland. Although many people think they should be called ponies because of their small stature, they are actually a kind of horse. These tough beasts are robust, strong, and very rarely get sick.

EMU

The emu is the world's second largest bird (after the ostrich). Its feathers are surprisingly soft, and its long legs end in three razor sharp claws. Emus can drink from 2.4 to 4.8 gallons of water a day!